W9-CKB-085

CRAWLING OUT THE WINDOW

Tom Hennen

CRAWLING OUT THE WINDOW

PROSE POEMS BY

TOM HENNEN

Black Hat Press
Goodhue, Minnesota
1997

Cover: *The Chicken House at Albert B. Myhre's Farm,* circa 1920, Spring Creek, Minnesota.

First printing, December 1997.

Printed and bound in the United States of America.
Design by Black Hat Press. (Goodhue, Minnesota).

Grateful acknowledgment is made to the editors of the following magazines for first publishing these poems:

Prairie Gate Press, "Crawling out the Window"; *1997 Minnesota Poetry Calendar,* "Looking for the Differences" and "Spring Evening in Prairie Woods"; *1998 Minnesota Poetry Calendar,* "Autumn Story"; and the anthology *Party Train: a Collection of North American Prose Poetry,* "Sheep in the Winter Night" and "Walking through a Narrow Strip of Woods."

Special thanks to Mark Vinz, Blue Cloud Abbey, and my parents, Ray and Kathleen Hennen.

ISBN 1-887649-04-2

Published and distributed by
Black Hat Press
Box 12
Goodhue, Minnesota 55027
612-923-4590

To Colleen, David, Aidan,
Matthew, and Sarah

Other books of poems by Tom Hennen

Love for Other Things

The Heron with No Business Sense

The Hole in the Landscape Is Real

Looking into the Weather

Selected Poems, 1963-1983

Contents

CRAWLING OUT THE WINDOW

CRAWLING OUT THE WINDOW

When water starts to run, winds come to the sky carrying parts of Canada, and the house is filled with the scent of dead grass thawing. When spring comes on the continental divide, the snowbanks are broken in two and half fall south and half fall north. It's the Gulf of Mexico or Hudson Bay, one or the other for the snow, the dirt, the grass, the animals and me. The Minnesota prairie has never heard of free will. It asks you, quietly at first, to accept and even love your fate. You find out that if you fall south, life will be easy, like warm rain. You wake up with an outgoing personality and a knack for business. The river carries you. You float easily and are a good swimmer. But if you fall north while daydreaming, you never quite get your footing back again. You will spend most of your time looking toward yourself and see nothing but holes. There will be gaps in your memory and you won't be able to earn a living. You always point north like a compass. You always have to travel on foot against the wind. You always think things might get better. You watch the geese and are sure you can fly.

THE ONE AND ONLY DAY

There has only ever been one day and it happens over and over. No one knows where it came from. It slides through time like the prow of a ship through sleeping water. It bumps against the shore of daylight each morning and sets sail alone in the dark at night. Sometimes under the awful glitter of stars. Sometimes into a thickly falling rain that sends the animals back to their dens and causes the woods to drip and become the color of owls.

A CHANGE OF WEATHER

First sunlight ripples on the grass and still water. Then the air is filled with flying seeds. Long mosquitoes rise like wind out of the hackles of the earth. The day brushes my cheek with a touch of cold fingers. Clouds leap in bunches from beneath the horizon and completely cover the ground like a dark thought. Rain begins first deep inside where I can smell the dust I'm made of.

GRASSLAND

Far south of the north woods, the red pine stands alone, surrounded by hundreds of miles of space, able to see a county away; it has been here for many years, its branches bent east by the wind. New grass grows in thin clumps close to its scaly trunk. Its long needles are green with spring. The landscape all around is bare hills and raw wind. Only close to the pine tree's bark is there the dim scent of forest, remote as a picture on a postcard. From the tree a sound of longing as the wind blows harder, and I know then that I've heard the sound of pining in its original voice, the singing within of those too much alone, when they are the only object on the horizon, sky on all sides, the day completely deserted, except for the sharp cold drops of rain that have started to fall.

AUTUMN MUSHROOMS

Autumn mushrooms are growing under the fallen leaves and sprouting from the trunks of rotting aspen trees. On the floor of the woods are strange gnarled roots. One looks like a swollen fist, brown and hairy, punching up out of the ground as if it were a detail in a fairy story about someone gathering firewood just as I am doing, frost shaking down on my boots from high grass, piling like snow on the leather toes, something from underground about to break through into the light, that will be talked about for years to come around a fireplace on sparkling cold nights when the winter is so long and the darkness so deep that the heart of the earth feels as if it might break.

SHAKING OFF THE NIGHT

Just before dawn the fields are asleep, the grass is bent with dew. Spruce trees are the first to lift themselves toward the frail light like a flock of forest-colored birds silently rising. Wind the only traffic, a gentle sound in the weeds. In the house people wake up and come back to themselves in the way animals out all night return to their dens. No one knows where the other has been.

WATERFOWL HUNTING SEASON

Autumn has come again to the fading garden behind the farmhouse. It has come with a wet day and thin, bare, shaking hardwood trees. The hunted ducks and geese have been scattered into the cold sky by gunshots. It's as though they are the dark words earth has written to draw down the snow that makes us happy when we least expect it, coming from nowhere, bright flakes swaying like tiny lanterns as they fall, leaving small drifts of light against the edges of the afternoon.

NIGHT STORM BY THE LAKE

From behind the hill full of heavy-leafed basswood the black storm clouds rise like the humped backs of buffalo. Over the tree tops they come, covering the evening light. Meanwhile, a slight breeze starts and lifts and falls in the long slough grass, quieting the mosquitoes. The lake cabin clutches the ground, its windows blinking. Over the hayfield there is a glow left by daylight. Night insects scatter as they look for shelter. Even the stones seem to dig down a little deeper where they lie. Cattails on the lake's edge shudder in a sudden wind. The first thick raindrops fall, throwing dust into the air as waves of darkness slap the shore.

SHEEP IN THE RAIN

All day dark rain has fallen on the white backs of the sheep where they stand under the oak trees. Water has soaked the branches and leaves. It penetrates the grass and dirt. It makes the rocks shine. The wet hours drip from the edge of the barn roof, each one darker than the last as night comes. The sheep are like lit-up windows or small piles of new snow. If they were not there the darkness would be complete.

CRICKETS IN THE DARK

The farmhouse I'm staying in this year is a hundred years old, big, with six bedrooms upstairs and a walk-in attic. I sleep in the living room by the open bay windows where the scent of cow manure and lilacs floats in from around the turn of the century, a simpler time of flowers and dust. I am so far out on the prairie that there are no lights except mine, the stars', and the fireflies'. When my lights are off, only the stars and the fireflies are left to show the earth which way to turn, while in the darkness the crickets leap into the deep end of night, singing.

TREE LIGHT AND TREE DARK

Wet aspen trees rock in some quiet rain dance no human can understand. The raindrops gleam in the gray day like transparent stones with their own source of light. The way plum leaves glow in autumn rain when everything else is so dark it can only be from light deep inside the soaked body of the tree.

Also, an odd thing happens on a day of sunshine when a dark woods approaches you. It may be only a clump of hand-planted evergreens on an open plain surrounded by air and light, but it pulls you inside to the cool damp of pine needles, your eyes resting with relief after bright sunlight, but also, a chill enters, like the lonesome thoughts of a suddenly homesick traveler.

PRAIRIE HEAT WAVE

Weather continues hot, baking the earth and its creatures. The sun breathes far away and we shudder, forgetting why, each of us a little sun ourselves passing across the day, breathing too, our mood changing every few minutes, sparks flying from our hair-tips like lightning striking the ground.

The day moves slowly as though under an anvil. The frightened smell of cut plants fills the afternoon as farmers chop alfalfa and sorghum. Trees cling to the earth like wood ticks to skin. The air is delirious with fear and heat and a stupor that lays things flat, letting the mind think only sexual thoughts.

Hand-planted pine trees are lined up in a row where I left them years ago, telling them not to move and they didn't, but now their young are growing, scattered around here and there with no order to their lives. Like the younger generation everywhere they are intoxicated by the scent of sunlight on their skin, and they shine like green islands in the dust.

THE LIFE OF A DAY

Like people or dogs, each day is unique and has its own personality quirks which can easily be seen if you look closely. But there are so few days as compared to people, not to mention dogs, that it would be surprising if a day were not a hundred times more interesting than most people. But usually they just pass, mostly unnoticed, unless they are wildly nice, like autumn ones full of red maple trees and hazy sunlight, or if they are grimly awful ones in a winter blizzard that kills the lost traveler and bunches of cattle. For some reason we like to see days pass, even though most of us claim we don't want to reach our last one for a long time. We examine each day before us with barely a glance and say, no, this isn't one I've been looking for, and wait in a bored sort of way for the next when, we are convinced, our lives will start for real. Meanwhile, this day is going by perfectly well-adjusted, as some days are, with the right amounts of sunlight and shade, and a light breeze scented with a perfume made from the mixture of fallen apples, corn stubble, dry oak leaves, and the faint odor of last night's meandering skunk.

WORDS IN THE WILD

Words are not common outdoors. Do you know how long it takes to find a word among the brush and tall prairie bluestem? You can look all morning and the word you need will be miles away resting under a windmill, soaking up sun. When you do catch the word it is rare and alive and does not want to be put into a pen or tossed inside a poem made like a large house. It needs to be left with open places around it, trusted enough not to be staked down. And still it sometimes runs off in the night.

SPRING EVENING IN PRAIRIE WOODS

I can hear the red-winged blackbirds calling, squawking as they do around a ripe cornfield, but it's still spring, the corn barely up. They make a chipping sound now that rises like a cloud of new dusk. In the woods across the road the grass is trying to be quiet because night is coming, while the long branches of the evergreen are lifting up the half moon as if it were a child.

TWO THINGS

After the winter there is a day full of spring wind
and on the plowing a small pond full of cold blue
water so clear that looking into it I regain con-
sciousness.

I wish it were different, but it is only when I am
alone that the pine tree will let its needles sur-
round me, shining, deep in its mental state of
abnormal well-being.

BY THE CREEK BANK

There is some secret that water holds that we need to know. I edge up close to the creek and peer into it for a revelation of some kind, an explanation of the world. Some things I think I know: that the sun rises, that the darkness heals, that animals are intelligent, that rocks are aware, that the earth has a sense of humor. The spring wind is blowing hard. The aspens along the bank make sounds of wood rubbing together like boards of an old house in a storm. Fair weather clouds break loose on the bottom of the western horizon and drift one by one across the blue sky. Below me in the creek there is a clear pool full of minnows. I get down on my belly and carefully put my hand into the water among the small fishes. The minnows jerk past my numb fingers like black seconds ticking. I cannot catch even one.

WHEN NIGHT NEARS

Light leaves the earth a piece at a time, one hand letting go of the tree branch while the other hangs on just a little longer, slowly losing its grip until it understands no help is coming and at last lets go. It falls into the darkness taking with it people and dogs, pine trees and butterflies, all the things we are so used to looking at in the daylight. It leaves the dark that feels like a body when you reach out, and the stars that glint so far off you wonder what they are good for.

TWO CROWS AND A JANUARY THAW

In deepest winter two crows throw their voices into the blue air. Toward the end of the thawing day they rise on the still-mild wind, two notes of music that have escaped the songbook. They drift out of sight and back again. Their rough calls float down light as shadows growing long. Soon in the dark pine grove the crows, like the night, will be silent, empty, waiting to fill with stars.

WINTER NAP

On a sunny winter afternoon I fill the stove with wood. When it is hot it makes the purring sound of the heart of a man revived after being dead for a few minutes. I pull a chair up to the heat, sit down with a book, and fall asleep. I leave my body and fly out over the snow-heavy fields. I sail about, avoiding tree tops, ignoring airplanes, gliding past sheds full of the cold metallic silence of tractors. I've always had to work with machines, be a machine, or less, part of a machine. Only those who don't need to earn their living chained to technology can afford to be romantic about it. The machine breaks down the nerves. Its rhythm is different than the rhythm of life. Its steel and plastic voice wedges itself between each beat of the heart. It throws the whole body off-center so that it can't digest moonlight or sunshine or understand a single chirping cricket. It makes it important to wake up from a winter nap to the smell of pine smoke, snow, and the light that comes in the frost-thick window, pale and soft as distant music.

A MAN TOO MUCH IN LOVE

The first woman who left him pushed him over a cliff. At least that's what it felt like when he landed two months later. She had come to him out of the warm afternoon, dark red hair and innocent face. In the air was the scent the ground has when it first opens up in spring, when all the birds become dizzy and some even drop dead with happiness.

The second woman who left him pulled all his teeth. At least that's what it felt like for two years and a day afterward. She had shining blond hair, a face that hit him like a bullet the first time he saw her. It was like seeing a birch tree alone on a hillside, its leaves yellow as a lamp in the rain.

The next woman who leaves him will find that he will get up each morning anyway. That he will fall in love once more with window sills and grasshoppers, with long-legged pine woods, and words that can be used over and over again in the moonlight.

THINGS ARE LIGHT AND TRANSPARENT

During the fall, objects come apart when you look at them. Farm buildings are mistaken for smoke among the trees. Stones and grass lift just enough off the ground so that you can see daylight under them. People you know become transparent and can no longer hide anything from you. The pond the color of the rainy sky comes up to both sides of the gravel road looking shiny as airplane wings. From it comes the surprised cry the heron makes each time it finds itself floating upward into a heaven of air, as if pulled by the attraction of an undiscovered planet.

ADRIFT IN WINTER

All anyone wants to know is when spring will get here. To hell with dripping icicles, cold blue snow, silly birds too dumb to go south, and sunlight gleaming off rock-hard snowflakes. I'm sick of breathing air sharp as razor blades. I'm tired of feet as hard to move as two buildings. I refuse to be seduced by the pine tree blocking my path. Even though . . . just now, look how it moves, its needles rubbing the sky-blue day. The glow it has around its entire body. How perfectly it stands in the snow-drift. The way both our shadows cross the noonhour at once, like wings.

OUT OF NOTHING

Snow began slowly. Only one flake fell all morning. It was talked about by everyone as they gathered for coffee. It brought back memories of other times. Dreams of ice skates, long shotguns waving at geese, cities lighting up somewhere off the prairie horizon in the cold gray day. Only one snowflake but it fell with the grace of a star out of the damp, ragged air. It filled the day with a clarity seldom noticed. It stood out sharply as a telephone pole against the skyline of the winter we each keep to ourselves.

MORE IDLENESS

It was one of those days. It was as if heat were rising from your body the way it does from the fields of wheat. You wanted to listen to endless conversation. The smell of the forest wound through the day like a sandy road. Your skin had the scent of sunshine. It was a day with no shadows. We lay in the long grass close to the pines. We both had the mediocre thoughts that people have in summer so that we became tolerant of even ourselves. The wonderful boredom went on and on while the afternoon pushed the horizon out of sight.

REPORT FROM THE WEST

Snow is falling west of here. The mountains have more than a foot of it. I see the early morning sky dark as night. I won't listen to the weather report. I'll let the question of snow hang. Answers only dull the senses. Even answers that are right often make what they explain uninteresting. In nature the answers are always changing. Like rain to snow, for instance. Nature can let the mysterious things alone—wet leaves plastered to tree trunks, the intricate design of fish guts. The way we don't fall off the earth at night when we look up at the North Star. The way we know this may not always be so. The way our dizziness makes us grab the long grass, hanging by our fingertips on the edge of infinity.

LANGUAGE

Almost a week of fog with frost that makes ghostly, monotonous days that drift out of the dark at dawn and back into it at dusk. Silence dense and woolly. The spruce trees white with splintery frost. Only the crows bring color to the day as they call to one another and walk the crusty snow, black eyes polished, beaks on the verge of human speech.

IN THE SKY OF WINTER

First day of winter and it seems all the insects are dead. None sail around any more or chirp or buzz or suddenly forget the art of flying above your soup. But they are there, under the leaves, burrowed into frozen plowing. Little wings folded, legs tucked close. They are in the tiny cases of their bodies, alive, some of them, but still as fallen twigs or stones. Meanwhile, the sky, lonesome without its tiny aviators, has filled the air with snowflakes.

LOOKING FOR THE DIFFERENCES

I am struck by the otherness of things rather than their sameness. The way a little pile of snow perches in the crook of a branch in the tall pine, away by itself, high enough not to be noticed by people, out of reach of stray dogs. It leans against the scaly pine bark, busy at some existence that does not need me.

It is the differences of objects that I love, that lift me toward the rest of the universe, that amaze me. That each thing on earth has its own soul, its own life, that each tree, each clod of dirt is filled with the mud of its own star. I watch where I step and see that the fallen leaf, old broken grass, an icy stone have placed themselves in exactly the right spot on the earth, carefully, like royalty in its own country.

AUTUMN'S DOOR

I have been following the seasons around and this one, autumn, is here again, new, turning the sumac red. The clouds are heavy autumn clouds that hang low and scud across the horizon, dragging their dark, ragged edges over the brightly lit grain stubble. Sometimes it's as though a door has opened into the landscape so that we can see clearly each leaf, the sharp outline of each prairie grass, and know for an instant just why we are here on this earth that is so loaded down with beauty it is about to tip over.

EARLY SPRING IN THE FIELD

The crow's voice filtered through the walls of the farmhouse sounds like a car engine turning over. Clouds on a north wind that whistles softly and cold. Spruce trees planted in a line on the south side of the house weave and scrape at the air. I've walked to a far field to a fence line of rocks where I am surprised to see soft mud this raw day. No new tracks in the mud, only desiccated grass among the rocks, a bare grove of trees in the distance, a blue sky thin as an eggshell with a crack of dark geese running through it, their voices faint and almost troubled as they disappear in a wedge that has opened at last the cold heart of winter.

HEAVEN HAS TWO SIDES

Frogs that sing in icy water on a sunny April morning know they are already in some kind of heaven. They tell us that the dimensions of one's body have nothing to do with the size of one's soul. Snakes are the other side of heaven, where praise is lazy and covered with sun-flecked scales on the warm edge of the rock pile, when we know that a fine spring day can curl and uncurl or disappear in the flick of a tongue.

MADE VISIBLE

The world is full of bodies. It's a happy thing and they should all be loved. Human bodies, raccoon bodies, blueberry and limestone bodies are the shapes we take when we want to be seen. How curious we are when we wake up and find ourselves in one of these new homes. The feel of snow, which we faintly remember, also the smell of wind, the sunshine's sweet taste. Sometimes I forget which body I'm in, like now, as I rest on my favorite log, an old aspen near Muddy Creek. The log, warm in the spring day, seems to lose more weight each year. It is dissolving as it dries. Before long it will be light enough to lift off the ground, rise past the tree tops and into the sky it loves so much, leaving behind the reminder that we are meant to spend our whole lives trembling in anticipation of the next instant.

PAIR-COUNTING WILD DUCKS AT WORK

I need a spring day to wake up. I've been nearly unconscious as an insect under the snow. In the warming days I move about from one thing to another, bumping into books, trees, rocks, house walls. In sunshine between rain showers I lie on a gravel hill above a duck pond. A box elder tree brushes my cheek with new leaves and I begin to thaw a little after the long winter. The leaves are warm as fur and touch me again and again in the quaking breeze. Sympathy is in the air, keeping me afloat on the day, as if I were one of the teal napping on the pond. I count the ducks, place their names in my notebook. I even count the broken cattails left from last year as they pass long hours away throwing clear reflections of themselves on the motionless water while they wait to be reborn.

TRACKING THE BREEZE

Deer tracks are easiest to identify, sunk in the mud along a cattail slough or cutting sharp hearts in new-fallen snow. Even the myopic amateur is certain of being correct about deer tracks. It's the other marks that cause you to lose your confidence. The long-fingered imprint of the raccoon makes you think of a strange child barefoot, on all fours, wandering the creek banks. Or the claws of a porcupine that poke holes in the soft ground far ahead of its footpads. Tracking in dry dirt or over hard ground is an act of faith. It depends on how well you pick up scents. How much you have learned from the soft night air when the coyote is out giving lessons to the sheep on how to survive on the odor of starlight.

GNATS

The autumn smell of earthworms has attracted an off-course migrating woodcock who explodes like a feathery fire cracker into the aspen thicket when I come too close. After all these nights of frost, most of the insects have given up for the year and have buried themselves in the duff with a few vague memories of sunshine. But here are tiny flies yet, small squadrons of them that dive and climb through the high reed grass. I don't know how these dark-eyed gnats have survived the cold beginning of fall. It is as if the autumn has a back door left open to a summer afternoon in the world next to ours.

SOMETHING IS HAPPENING

Uphill I see the rim of sky. The cold wind urgently talks in several voices at once as though something serious is happening. Clouds push hard on those of us caught between them and the floor of the earth. The wet snow turns grass and ground white, but the water of the small lake is warm, a dark tongue on which snow melts. In the willow thickets a knocking of branches together, as if something on the other side wants to get in.

THE ANT MOUND

Those fall days are best when the afternoons warm up enough to take the edge off, and my ragged work jacket is too heavy, but I leave it on anyway. In the old gravel pit I take a break from cutting wood. Aspen and cottonwood have grown up since the pit was abandoned. Some have become real trees and show their age with broken limbs and lightning scars. Under the shivering yellow leaves there is a large ant mound with only a few big ants on it. They have sealed it against the coming winter and now make one last check for open holes. I cannot see how they will be able to get back in. I wonder if they have sacrificed themselves for the others. They are calm. When they stop to rest, the sunlight seems to give them pleasure. I sit beside them for a long time while we feel sorry for the ones safely inside.

SHEEP IN THE WINTER NIGHT

Inside the barn the sheep were standing, pushed close to one another. Some were dozing, some had eyes wide open listening in the dark. Some had no doubt heard of wolves. They looked weary with all the burdens they had to carry, like being thought of as stupid and cowardly, disliked by cowboys for the way they eat grass about an inch into the dirt, the silly look they have just after shearing, of being one of the symbols of the Christian religion. In the darkness of the barn their woolly backs were full of light gathered on summer pastures. Above them their white breath was suspended like the soul each one surely had, while far off in the pine woods, night was deep in silence. The owl and rabbit were wondering, along with the trees, if the air would soon fill with snowflakes, but the power that moves through the universe and makes our hair stand on end was keeping the answer to itself.

ALL SOULS' DAY

I'm in the tall grass on an autumn day, deep among the small hills far from any towns or farms. The aspen trees drop their last dead leaves. Wind rises from plum brush as if letting out a long-held breath. It is a lonesome sound, as though made by someone a little depressed. The sounds now are fewer than in summer. So many birds gone God knows where. Insects only shells left behind, their bodies food for their spirits on the journey to the afterlife. To think they will be waiting for us when we get there—mosquitoes, blackflies—like old friends who annoy us but we can't shake, any more than we can shake our own personalities which hum inside us like bees, happy with even the least cold sunlight.

SOAKING UP SUN

Today there is the kind of sunshine old men love, the kind of day when my grandfather would sit on the south side of the wooden corncrib where the sunlight warmed slowly all through the day like a wood stove. One after another dry leaves fell. No painful memories came. Everything was lit by a halo of light. The cornstalks glinted bright as pieces of glass. From the fields and cottonwood grove came the damp smell of mushrooms, of things going back to earth. I sat with my grandfather then. Sheep came up to us as we sat there, their oily wool so warm to my fingers, like a strange and magic snow. My grandfather whittled sweet smelling apple sticks just to get at the scent. His thumb had a permanent groove in it where the back of the knife blade rested. He let me listen to the wind, the wild geese, the soft dialect of sheep, while his own silence taught me every secret thing he knew.

BACKPACKING AMONG THE THISTLES

A cold June morning at work. I am out in the country spraying Canada thistles with the chemical 2, 4-D. Who can I tell who won't consider me a villain, a herbicidist, a ravager of the earth? The marsh is full of wildly singing birds. Soon the sun will warm things up. I have on a metal backpack sprayer full of water and poison as I move deep into the high thistles. Mosquitoes cover my face, fill my eyes and ears. The straps pull me down as I walk. I can hear someone a mile away firing a rifle at short intervals. There is a tractor noise far off. Near me red-winged blackbirds are shrill and annoyed. Wind rises and falls in the grass, air brushes the tips of plants along the water, and causes the weeds to hum to themselves.

AFTER FALLING INTO THE SLOUGH IN EARLY SPRING

Back in the water, my clothes beginning to dry out, I listen to the light wind in the small bare cottonwood trees on shore. I stand there for a long time, until the teal start to swim close, a marsh wren tries to land on me, and the cricket frogs start up their calls that sound like pebbles hitting together. I scoop up one of the tiny frogs that floats by on an old leaf and hold him by his hind legs just tight enough to silence his singing. His dark eyes have no fear in them. His body is no more than an inch long and brown as tobacco but less useful—luckily for him. He waits patiently for me to be done with him. I know I'll never see him again once I let him go so I hold on a little longer. If nature has a soul, this tiny frog could be the shape it takes. And if that soul makes a noise, it might sound like small stones being hit together. I don't know when I will again find something so innocent, with a heart I can feel beating quietly as melting snow.

LEAVING AND RETURN

How long the rain falls. It throws itself from the black sky wrapped around a tiny piece of dirt. The trees shake their leaves with a sound like wet glass breaking. Light from the window is smeared against the night. To the spring wind we are nothing but dust it could carry off if it wanted. It could lift us into the clouds where we would have to wait until we became the center of the raindrop, and then, some dark day, we would leap toward earth and the roof of a well-lit house.

WHAT THE PLANTS SAY

Tree, give up your secret. How can you be so satisfied? Why don't you need to change location, look for a better job, find prettier scenery or even want to get away from people?

Grass, you don't care where you turn up. You appear running wild in the oat field, out of a crack in a city street. You are the first word in the vocabulary of the earth. How is it that you are able to grow so near the lake without falling in? How can you be so alert for the early frost, bend in the slightest breeze, and yet be so hard to break that you are still there, quiet, green, among the ruins of others?

Weed, it is you with your bad reputation that I love the most. Teach me not to care what anyone has to say about me. Help me to be in the world for no purpose at all except for the joy of sunlight and rain. Keep me close to the edge where everything wild begins.

OUTSIDE WORK

On these autumn days when even the sunshine is cold, I feel like the wild bee that comes looking for one last flower before the snow. I move like the bee, drowsily through the warm spots in the day. My muscles, too, are stiff if I drift into the shadows. The sudden chill makes me shudder and I move like someone swimming through the floating spider webs. I reach a clearing in the sunlight where the earth itself seems about to fall asleep into its own daydream. In the dream the bee and I are both children in the same family. We have never left home. Everything we touch tastes like honey.

ON THE FAR PRAIRIE

A grove of trees lies lightly as cloud shadow on the prairie in the sunny fall afternoon. Seen closer, a spruce tree pokes sharp as an arrow above the dark patch on the sunlit horizon. Old cottonwoods can be made out, along with the outline of a barn and silo. The outbuildings and the places they occupy among the grove make the farmstead look like a fortress in the wilds. The tall spruce could have a flag snapping from its top to identify another stronghold temporarily taken. In the remote and overwhelming landscape of the cosmos it cannot be held for long. But now, in the honey-scented autumn, the mysterious emptiness that surrounds us seems touched by our efforts and rocks us from one season to another through a century of perfect days.

WHEN STORMS COME

When a great thunderstorm comes out of the southwest, rolling dark over the grassland with crackling white lightning that strikes as close as your hair, then all the things made by humans become small, and all the things we have learned take up almost no room at all. Towns are perfectly still. Farm buildings disappear among the rain-shiny groves of cottonwood trees. In the farmhouse we are quiet. In the barn doorway we don't move, thinking we won't be seen, while the earth rocks, and the lightning seeks to touch—like a tap on the shoulder—its next partner for the dance.

WALKING THROUGH A NARROW STRIP OF WOODS

Pines as always pried at the sky with their tips, ignoring the wind around their trunks. I dodged the stinging underbrush as it was snapped off. Sometimes a branch would hit my cheek. I thought for an instant how ungrateful nature is. I noticed how my boots crunched the new thin snow, pushing the flakes together. I remembered the last time I was in the city. How the grass grew in the sidewalk. How the spruce tree was still standing in the morning next to the parked car. How the singing coming from within the tree might not have been birds, that the thread nature uses to connect all things together is joy. When I think of this in a narrow woods I fill with shame for all the cruel things I've said about cities, for they too, will dissolve as bones dissolve, as the rain is broken by the ground, and because we are allowed to pity everything except ourselves.

Carol Orban

TOM HENNEN works as an outdoor laborer and sometimes as a seasonal Wildlife Biological Technician. He has two grown children and a grandson.